05/07

Countries of the World

Ireland

by Kathleen W. Deady

Consultants:
Phyllis Brugnolotti
Assistant Librarian
American Irish Historical Society

David A. Fleming
University of Limerick, Republic of Ireland

Bridgestone Books
an imprint of Capstone Press
Mankato, Minnesota

Bridgestone Books are published by Capstone Press
151 Good Counsel Drive, P.O. Box 669, Mankato, Minnesota 56002
http://www.capstone-press.com

Library of Congress Cataloging-in-Publication Data
Deady, Kathleen W.
   Ireland/by Kathleen W. Deady.
   p. cm.—(Countries of the world)
   Includes bibliographical references and index.
   ISBN 0-7368-0814-0
   1. Ireland—Juvenile literature. [1. Ireland.] I. Title. II. Countries of the world (Mankato, Minn.)
DA906 .D43 2001
941.7—dc21   00-009729

Summary: Discusses the landscape, culture, food, animals, sports, and holidays of Ireland.

Editorial Credits
Erika Mikkelson, editor; Karen Risch, product planning editor; Linda Clavel, production
   designer and illustrator; Katy Kudela, photo researcher

Photo Credits
Carl Purcell/Pictor, cover
Kay Shaw, 6, 10, 16
Maggi Moetell, 12
Richard Cummins, 8
Root Resources/Kenneth Rapalee, 18
StockHaus Limited, 5 (top)
Unicorn Stock Photos/Jeremy Bisley, 14; Jim Shippee, 20

1 2 3 4 5 6 06 05 04 03 02 01

Table of Contents

Fast Facts

Name: Republic of Ireland
Capital: Dublin
Population: More than 3.7 million
Languages: English, Gaelic
Religion: Mostly Roman Catholic

Size: 27,135 square miles
(70,280 square kilometers)
Ireland is slightly larger than the U.S. state of West Virginia.
Crops: Wheat, barley, potatoes

Maps

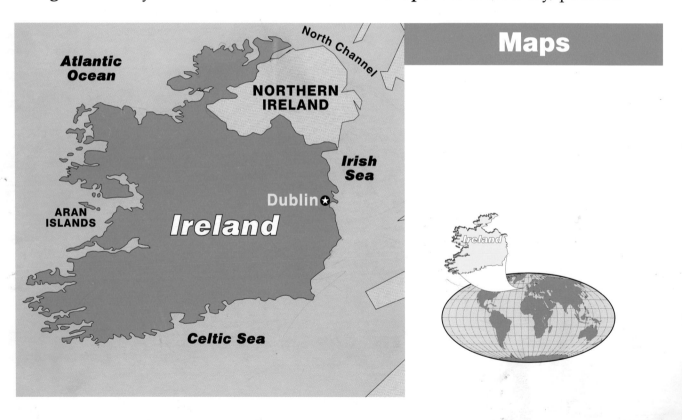

Atlantic Ocean

North Channel

NORTHERN IRELAND

Irish Sea

ARAN ISLANDS

Ireland

Dublin ✪

Celtic Sea

Ireland

Flag

Ireland's flag has three vertical stripes. The stripes are green, white, and orange. Green stands for the Catholics in Ireland. Orange stands for the Protestants. White is for the hope of unity between the Catholics and Protestants. Ireland officially adopted the flag on December 29, 1937.

Currency

The unit of currency in Ireland is the Irish punt, or pound. One hundred pence equal one Irish pound.

In 2000, about 80 pence equaled one U.S. dollar. About 56 pence equaled one Canadian dollar.

The Land

Ireland lies on an island in northwestern Europe. The Republic of Ireland takes up about five-sixths of the island. Northern Ireland occupies the rest of the island. The Irish Sea on the east separates Ireland from Great Britain. Great Britain and Northern Ireland make up the United Kingdom. The Atlantic Ocean borders Ireland on the northwest, west, and south.

Ireland's landscape varies. Rolling pastures and rich farmlands cover central and southern Ireland. This region has many lakes, bogs, and rivers. Low mountains and rugged hills rise along the coastal areas.

Ireland's climate is damp and mild. This wet climate makes Ireland's land green. Ireland is nicknamed the Emerald Isle. Some people think Ireland looks like a beautiful green jewel.

People call Ireland the Emerald Isle because of its lush, green land.

Life at Home

About 60 percent of Irish people live in cities or towns. Most people live in the east and south. Some people rent apartments called flats. Many others own their homes.

Modern houses are made of brick or concrete. Most houses have four to seven rooms. Some families also have summer houses for vacations. A few people still live in traditional stone and mortar cottages with thatched roofs. People no longer build these types of homes.

Family bonds are important to the Irish. Most families have two or three children. Many women stay home to care for their children. Other family members such as grandparents or unmarried aunts or uncles often live in the house too.

Families enjoy social activities together. Some go to local pubs where they eat and drink, talk and listen to music.

Some people live in cottages with thatched roofs.

Going to School

All Irish children must attend school from ages 6 to 15. The Catholic Church runs most elementary schools in Ireland. Irish children attend school from September to June. They have vacations at Christmas and Easter.

Students attend elementary school up to age 12. They study reading, math, and other subjects in English. Students also study Irish culture. They learn traditional stories, music, and crafts. All Irish children also learn to speak and write Gaelic.

Secondary schools offer several areas of study. Students can choose a general education to prepare for college. They also may take vocational classes. These classes teach skills for many jobs.

Students receive a Junior Certificate at age 15 or 16. They may continue school for two more years. Students then receive a Leaving Certificate. They then can go to a university or technical college.

Many Irish schools are for only girls or only boys.

Irish Food

Irish food is simple and healthy. The Irish grow and eat many fruits and vegetables. Many people in Ireland like to eat potatoes. Dairy products like milk and butter are popular. Tea is the most common drink.

A traditional Irish breakfast usually is large. The meal includes eggs, as well as bacon, sausage, and other meats. Tomatoes, hot cereal, and Irish soda bread also are common. People make Irish soda bread with baking soda and buttermilk. Many people eat smaller breakfasts today.

Most Irish main dishes include beef, chicken, mutton, or pork. Irish stew is famous. It is mutton or pork boiled with potatoes, onions, and herbs. Bacon, cabbage, and potatoes also are favorites. The Irish enjoy smoked salmon and Irish lamb too. Popular Irish desserts include tarts and cakes.

Breakfast often includes eggs, sausage, and tomatoes.

Animals

Ireland has fewer mammals than the rest of Europe. Mammals are warm-blooded animals with a backbone. Only 31 species of mammals live in the country. The Irish stoat and the Irish hare are common. Red deer, foxes, and red squirrels live throughout Ireland. Otters thrive in the bog lands. Two types of mice live in the woods and fields.

Ireland has many water animals. Salmon, trout, char, and pollan swim in the rivers and lakes. Cod, haddock, herring, and lobster are abundant in the coastal waters.

Ireland has no snakes. The common lizard is the only reptile. The only amphibians are a kind of frog, a toad, and a newt.

About 380 different species of birds live in Ireland. Ducks, geese, swans, and waders live in the inland waters. Merlin fly over the coastal areas to hunt their prey.

Foxes eat small animals such as rabbits.

Crafts and Music

Ireland is famous for many arts and crafts. Women of the Aran Islands off the mainland coast make hand-knit wool sweaters. People value Irish lace, linens, and tweeds for their beauty. Tweeds are wool fabrics with two or more colors woven together.

Many other crafts also are popular. Tourists buy Irish-made musical instruments, candles, and pottery. Belleek china and Waterford crystal are famous. Waterford crystal is made in the coastal town of Waterford.

Irish music is popular around the world. Musicians play lively traditional songs at parties. These parties are called ceilidhs (KAY-lees).

Traditional instruments are important to Irish music. Uilleann (IH-lehn) pipes are well known. Bellows power these small bagpipes. A bodhran (BAW-rahn) is a small, hand-held drum. Other instruments include flutes and the Celtic harp.

Sweaters made on the Aran Islands are world famous.

Sports and Games

Irish people enjoy many sports. The ancient game of hurling is a national favorite. This fast game is similar to field hockey. Players use a small leather ball and a hurley, or caman. They use this curved stick to hurl the ball through the opponent's goalpost. Camogie is the women's version of hurling.

Gaelic football also is popular. It is a mix of soccer and rugby. Other favorite sports in Ireland include soccer, rugby, cricket, and boxing.

Horseracing is a national pastime. Ireland has about 30 racetracks. The Derby is Ireland's most famous horse race. It is held at Kildare County's Curragh racecourse in late June. The Irish Grand National is held near Dublin on the Monday after Easter.

Irish people enjoy a variety of relaxing activities. They go cycling, play golf, or sail. Others relax with friends and play chess, bingo, or bridge.

The Killarney races take place in mid-July.

Holidays and Celebrations

Saint Patrick's Day on March 17 is Ireland's biggest national holiday. Saint Patrick taught Christianity to the Irish. Cities hold parades. Dublin has the largest parade and fireworks display in the country.

Easter is an important Christian holiday. People light hundreds of small candles in church. Families spend a quiet day at home. Roast lamb is a common Easter meal.

Christmas is a special family time. People decorate their homes with holly and ivy. They put candles in their windows and attend church.

Saint Stephen's Day or Wren Day is December 26. Years ago, people thought the wren was a sacred bird. Today, young men sometimes dress in costumes and paint their faces. They go from house to house with a dead wren looking for money to bury it.

People wear green on Saint Patrick's Day.

Hands On: Pass the Orange

Players most often use an orange in this Irish team game. You can use any similar object of about the same size.

What You Need

Enough players for two teams
Two oranges

What You Do

1. Divide the players into two teams. Line up each team in a single line.
2. Give the first player on each team an orange. This player places the orange under his or her chin.
3. Have someone give a signal to start. The first player in each line passes the orange to the second player. Players may use only their chin and neck to pass the orange. They may not use their hands.
4. A team must start again if a player drops the orange.
5. Each team continues to pass the orange from player to player. The first team to pass the orange to the end of their line wins.

Learn to Speak Gaelic

Irish Gaelic has many sounds not found in American English. The alphabet has 18 of the 26 letters of the English alphabet. It does not have the letters j, k, q, v, w, x, y, and z.

good bye	slan agat	(slawn AH-gut)
hello	dia dhuit	(JEE-ah ghwich)
how are you	conas ta tu	(KUN-us taw too)
please	le do thoil	(LED heuyl)
thank you	go raibh maith agat	(guh ro moh AH-gut)

Words to Know

amphibian (am-FIB-ee-uhn)—an animal that can live on land or in water; amphibians go through tadpole and adult life stages.

bellows (BEL-ohz)—a device that forces air out when its sides are pushed together

bog (BAWG)—a wet, spongy area of land

Christianity (kriss-chee-AN-uh-tee)—the religion based on the life and teachings of Jesus Christ

isle (EYE-uhl)—an island

pub (PUHB)—a bar where adults can drink alcohol

stoat (STOHT)—a weasel-like animal with a short tail

thatched (THACHD)—made of straw

tradition (truh-DISH-uhn)—a custom, an idea, or a belief that is handed down from one generation to the next

Read More

Bell, Rachael. *A Visit to Ireland.* A Visit To. Des Plaines, Ill.: Heinemann Library, 1999.

January, Brendan. *Ireland.* A True Book. New York: Children's Press, 1999.

Kent, Deborah. *Dublin.* Cities of the World. New York: Children's Press, 1997.

Useful Addresses and Internet Sites

Embassy of Ireland
2234 Massachusetts Avenue NW
Washington, DC 20008

Embassy of Ireland
130 Albert Street
Ottawa, Ontario K1P 5G4
Canada

Embassy of Ireland, Washington, DC
http://www.irelandemb.org
The World Factbook 2000—Ireland
http://www.odci.gov/cia/publications/factbook/geos/ei.html

Index